To Gail a
that you
with lots of love
Jack Scheu

Also by Jack Schwarz

Finding

The

Jewel

In The

Molasses

Finding the
Jewel
in the
Molasses

Master
These Words of Wisdom

by
Jack Schwarz

Schwarz Publishing · *Grants Pass, Oregon* · *1996*

Schwarz Publishing
515 N.E. 8th Street
Grants Pass, OR 97526

Cover design and art work by Diane Fassler Chasmar
Text design by Michael Clark
Printing services by Central Printing

LIBRARY OF CONGRESS CATALOGING-IN-PUBLICATION DATA
Schwarz, Jack, 1924-
Finding the Jewel in the Molasses

[1. Self-help. 2. Mind and Body. 3. Health. 4. Natural
immunity-Psychological aspects.] I. Title
96-69619 ISBN 1-887417-01-X

First Printing 1996
Manufactured in the United States of America

Acknowledgments

My many thank yous to the teamwork and cooperation that made possible *Finding the Jewel in the Molasses.*

My acknowledgment to Jim Sours, Nancy and Don Ingram, Margie Kuehn, Tom Blamer, Helen Wallace, Joy Craddick, Buddy Frumker, Regina Marga, Bernice Sage, and Sandra D'Angela for all their creativity and sensitivity in preparing this work.

My special appreciation to my partner in life, Lois, for her steadfast love and dedication.

This book is dedicated
to all Aletheia Interns

DANGER!

When you read this book,
you may lose your two best friends...

IGNORANCE

&

AVOIDANCE

Jack Schwarz

CONTENTS

FOREWORD

Last week, my youngest son, Michael, put his book down, looked rather reflective, and said, "You know, Dad, this is the best book I have ever read. As a matter of fact, if there were only one book in the world, it should be this one. It tells us everything we would ever need to know."

This week, I read *"Finding the Jewel in the Molasses "* by Jack Schwarz, as he put together the pages to be sent to the publisher, and I felt the same way.

In ancient days, long before there was a written language and scribes were kept on the payroll to record the stories of human development, the storyteller was an important part of the community. Storytellers wandered through the lands, providing the population with a magic window through which they could view not only the history of their ancestors, but could begin to understand their own inner psychology and destiny.

Often, people would travel for days to hear the stories about life that flowed, like the crystal droplets that form pure mountain streams, from the lips of the gifted elder who had committed to memory the stories from the past, or could call up, through visions, parables that worked like salve to ease the pains of a life of toil and hardship.

Today, we are still blessed with those gifted story-tellers that not only see the truth as it exists in the Universe, but have the ability to put the truth into metaphors that we can easily understand. Now, with the advent of the printed page, we no longer need travel farther than our local bookstores or public libraries to sate our hunger for words. Through the reading of books we can ease our life of relationships and look through the magic windows that show us the way to taste the sweet nectar and the bitter gall forming the cycles of our lives.

Have you ever wondered that the human form comes into this world without even a simple sheet of mimeographed instructions? Even our VCR comes with a manual that, if followed, will provide for years of maximum service. We are fortunate that no manual exists for us, because if we followed it, we would experience a lifetime of lukewarm temperatures while we traveled a perfectly level terrain. It is the *experience* of life that gives us the excitement and the changes that hurtle us from the freezing temperatures at the mountain peak, to the searing heat on the low lying floor of the desert.

Rather than an owner's manual, this is a manual for optimum participation in the Earthly domain: a system for enhancing performance, health and interactions.

All of our lives we have been bombarded with homilies to the point where we hear more information than we care to listen to. As a result we hear words constantly, but we do not *know* the experiences behind the words. We are so accomplished at intellectual pursuit that we have become practically barren of *knowing*.

Knowing is the state where we have experienced an event and carry with us the authority to say, "This is my experience. No matter how you feel, or what you believe, I *know* this is the way I have experienced life." We no longer need to rely on someone else for our confirmations. We may not be able to explain what we know, but it is at a cellular level of existence and becomes noticeable in our actions.

The words in this book are of no value. From the most ancient teachings to the most modern, the true masters have always said, "Do not listen to my words. Be immersed in my energy. Feel me. It is by my energy that you will understand, not through my words." Sri Auribindo says that you cannot relate to anything you do not know about and you cannot know anything unless you can become it.

If, after reading a poem, or one of the statements taken from Jack's lectures, we begin to live the experience symbolized by the words, we will begin to enhance performance, health, and interaction. There is only one way to get full value from the information included in the pages of this book. It is to perceptualize the meaning behind the words, experiment with incorporating the idea into our daily life, be consciously aware of the experience, and then use that knowing to enhance our own life, which will in turn enhance everything in the Universe.

There is one statement we will come to shortly that tells us that ignorance is a result of our habits. Another tells us not to Re-act. These two, habits and reaction, cause us to stay stuck in our present form of behavior. That is fine. No one is suggesting that we change from the present situation, but, if we are interested in a different life, we must begin to deal with habit and re-action.

Jack tells us that if we learn to use our ability to *respond* from the heart and not *react* from the solar plexus in each new situation we can engineer our own genetic structure, which will provide us the opportunity to increase our radiance rather than stagnate the flow of our energy. An example follows of how we get confused about the importance of, or maybe the lack of importance we give to words. Even though many people would not consider eating the menu below:

MENU
Pepperoni
Pizza
Macaroni
Salad
Pumpkin Pie
Whipped Cream

We do so in our daily experiences. We do not live the flavor of the messages we receive. If someone tells us to, *Do unto others as you would have others do unto you*, we say, "Oh, that is nice. I believe that," and then we build bigger bombs; bully those we think are weaker or lesser than we; and break up relationships with behaviors that are less than endearing to our partners.

We only need to understand that most of us will eat the menu instead of holding out for the flavor of the actual food. That is "eating the menu." We are satisfied that the words are more important than what they symbolize.

Jack Schwarz is the story teller in this book who will provide the reader with insights into life as it was intended to be lived—a life of missions and service—a life of risks and consequences. And through all the poems and statements, you are provided the opportunity to experiment and search for the individual truths that are called *knowing*.

All of these statements and poems were selected from years of lectures and classes presented by Jack Schwarz of the *Aletheia H.E.A.R.T. Institute* on Mendicino, California. Jack is considered a great teacher, but that is not an accurate description. Jack is a great *learner*. A learner is someone who makes personal changes in his/her life based on cognition of experiences and events. For over sixty years, Jack has put his body where his mouth is. Many teachers will tell a person, *do as I say, not as I do. Jack will say*, "I did this and it worked for me. You experiment with it and see if it is universal in its scope."

If you were to question any of the statements, you would only need to look at the model, and see that it is an accurate statement for Jack. As you work through this manual, you will find that we are to become models of the statements. If you do not, they are meaningless. You might as well eat the menu.

As you begin to experiment with the poems and statements in your daily life, watch what you become. This is a time for you to do a self-evaluation of your own progress and your interactions with your environment.

As you read through the book, you will probably say to yourself, "Gosh, that is simple. I knew that." And you would be correct in your thinking. The trick is, though, to incorporate the statement into your beingness so that anyone you meet will know from your actions.

You have ahead of you a rare opportunity to sit with the master and to drink in the energy.

Don Ingram

Denial of Spirit

What is meant by "denial of spirit"? This cannot be intellectualized; it must come from the heart. To think about it is to deny the spirit. Denial means that we view as tragic all of the tremendous transitions and problems occurring in the world, rather than understanding that these are continuous processes of growth in our lives. They are the challenges which show how much spirit we have!

How much are we utilizing spirit rather than seeing the problems as tragedies? We need to begin celebrating spirit as a process state which flows through our lives at all times. When we deny spirit, our blocks become greater blocks and our barricades become huge barricades. Denial of spirit causes us to become more and more fragmented.

We have not always recognized what we mean by "spirit" and have often used that word loosely. To me, the soul is the container which has the allocated energy of each individual within it. This essence within the container is what I call spirit. The spirit is different from any other energy in the Universe because it is pure essence. It has not been diluted and it has not been adulterated. Spirit is what our real truth is all about.

If we deny spirit, we also deny faith. In this instance we are only giving credit to our human capacities to understand life, rather than having the understanding come from within, from the heart and soul. So denial of spirit is denial of our own truth! We get so stuck in the physical aspects of this life and all its problems that we do not realize that there is one answer for everything and that is intuitive inspirational thought.

Right now I would like you to take a deep breath, to let it come in. This act of inspiring is actually taking in new life. Now as you breathe out, exhale all your sorrows and all your pain, which have been transformed by your breath. These energies now sparkle and have become, indeed, radiant. As you exhale, become excited! Do not worry if it is OK or not OK. By expressing freely, an excitement takes place which penetrates every cell of your being. Your radiance picks up a much higher power and nothing of a lower power can affect it. Many of us go by belief systems rather than by knowing systems. For example, when we have an experience, we start to analyze and question. What should be done and how should it be done? Why is it happening? How does it come about? Rather than questioning, we need to allow the experience to go on. Knowledge is indeed good to have; the intellect needs to be given as much credit as we give the intuition. However, the intellect is only confirming what we already know.

You see, if we believe and know that God is omnipotent, we also have to recognize God's omnipresence, God is present in all. But we have to bring this knowing into a knowing of spirit, instead of denying spirit. Recognize your denial and look at it as an "ah hah" experience.

When we get this "ah hah" feeling, we say it is

happening to us. We cannot start checking it out if the experience is or is not working for us, for we do not have the wisdom yet to know how the destiny of life should be. To some extent, to look ahead and to perceive what one needs to do in the coming times, to think and analyze, again we are denying the spirit. We do not have the faith that things are going to go in the way they should go.

When I look in my own life, there are many things which I certainly have not chosen intellectually to be involved in. I have gone through experiences in my life which really would have made me give up everything. And instead of giving faith to God and faith to the inner spirit, I could have said that I did not deserve that as so many of us do. We do everything so well, and suddenly, there we are, struck by situations that seemingly we do not deserve. It is because we do not feel we deserve it, that we start to deny spirit.

In addition to omnipresence and omnipotence, we also have to have omniscience which means the all knowingness. We forget that we are representatives of this omniscient energy field. As an individualized allocation of that God-given spirit, we need to express omniscience in all aspects of our lives. This does not happen at just a certain time of day. The spirit must be allowed to come through continuously. This will give us the courage to face all the challenges in life. There are more challenges in life. There are more challenges all the time. The circumstances in this life are causing many of us confusion as to what to do. We need to trust that spirit will come through and give us the answers rather than searching for answers and doing all kinds of things in order to bring about a certain outcome. This only blocks us more and more.

One of the biggest problems in this day and age is lack of self-esteem. This is another sign of denial of spirit. Only spirit gives you esteem and the understanding of your own potentials. Your potentials are there for you to express. You cannot compare yourself with other beings. Many times I say to people that in your body are 750 trillion cells, give or take a couple of trillion, and although many cells are similar, each is unique. How, then can you be the same as another being if you have 750 trillion *unique* cells in your body? There is no point in comparing yourself with other people because you are not exactly like them. You are unique, with unique potentials. Your job is to develop all your gifts and talents. If you do not do this, you are denying spirit and not allowing it to work in your life.

I am a very competitive person. However, I compete with no one but myself. I go for the statement in the scriptures that says "the best is yet to be." If you deny spirit, you will never see the best. Realize that the best for now is not good enough for two seconds from now.

Another denial is the continuous lament about what we cannot do. "I cannot do this, this is not the right time," and so forth. This all arises from the thinking process that denies that you have the ability to do it. When you are challenged to *act* upon something, you *react* instead. Immediately you say, "I cannot do this."

I am never satisfied. I call myself a "very dissatisfied-content person." By this paradox I mean that I am not satisfied with anything I do, or say, or accomplish because satisfaction means immediately putting the brakes on and resting on my laurels. It means that I think I have "made it" when actually I have not. I have just finished one particular aspect or one cycle of things.

In their struggles with all kinds of things, many people lament their dissatisfaction. They go to their cosmic wailing walls. Instead they could say "Ah Hah! I have achieved that. It is not yet the best, but it is the best I could do for now." Granting yourself this gratification and contentment brings forth one of the highest states of your being which is joy—not pleasure, but *joy*. You then have the ability to say "I am content with what I did but I am dissatisfied because it could be better." Now you are already taking the next challenge. You are looking at the challenge instead of blocking it.

Most of the diseases we talk about, no matter what labels we give them, come forth from not allowing ourselves to be joyful. We deny that we have abilities even though we all come to be representatives of this creative force called "God." God is omnipotent. Why then do we deny these powers? Is the drop in the ocean less powerful than the ocean? Only quantitatively, but qualitatively it has the same qualities as the whole ocean. You have the same qualities as the total universe and everything that God has created in this universe. You as an individual have a unique function. You can bring out the best, knowing that the best is yet to be.

I was never told what the best is. Look at how much energy we put into false perfection, yet we do not know what perfection is. What we call perfection is not what others would call it. I have often joked about perfection being a carrot that God has hanging in front of your nose. Every time you think you have it, it has moved a couple of feet in front of you and you have to aim at it again. We may never know what perfection is in this physical life because it lies within the Universal Beingness; actually, as we say, sitting next to God.

Become Godlike, no matter what form that takes, whether the human form or the form after this form. For myself, I do not want to think about the next form because I have enough problems with this form. If I start looking ahead, I am not going to be at ease with this form. Quite often those who cannot handle the present form start to create what I call "cellular suicide." When we block our true nature and hold back our spontaneity we are denying spirit. This causes improper functioning of the body and creates cellular suicide.

Recognize that the body is a vehicle through which the spirit has to act. If you give more power to the malfunction of this physical instrument, you will suffer more by denying the spirit. You do not see that healing does not come from the outside. The healing comes from within. Do not identify and hang yourself up on these denials.

Introduction

We can overcome the state of human despair. Recognize that the essence of joy is hidden in every despair. I always remember what Kahil Gibran says in *The Prophet* when the woman asked him about joy. The master answered, "Your joy of today is your suffering of yesterday unmasked." We get so engrossed in suffering that we forget that we have to go through suffering in order to discover joy.

We are aware of many sayings, but we do not always live them. We say, "Every cloud has a silver lining," but we still keep emphasizing the dark clouds. This emphasis denies spirit. We need to start living in an exciting way. We need to enter into light with the faith that we can overcome all struggles if we stay in a blessed state. I really feel that I have been blessed tremendously in my life by all the obstacles.

Obstacles have shown me my attachments and where I need to let go. Most of us have not understood the famous statement "Let go and let God." Sometimes we let go and then sit around and wait for God to do everything. We forget that when God created us he gave us all the tools to do it ourselves. Letting go simply means letting go of all our attachments. All your habits, addictions, and attachments come from lack of understanding and denial of your spirit. They need to be transmuted and recycled and returned to nature.

What about going back to nature? You can recycle your bottles and your aluminum cans, but if you do not recycle all your attachments, you are still working only on one level and the other levels are not being touched.

We need to start saying, "I am a blessed person. I lost this or that, but it opens up new opportunities for me to learn; a new lesson can begin; I am ready to step into the new lesson." A few times in my life I lost everything that I materially possessed. What an opportunity! I must not have needed it anymore. Now I have the opportunity to start working to gather it again and never to become so attached to it. I live more easily now. If it is done, it is gone—another opportunity to grow. It can be uplifting.

The same thing is true about all your mental aspects. You lack self-esteem because you have not given credit to all your potentials. You deny the spirit. Let us at this moment take a vow to ourselves and higher Self that we are going to allow spirit to speak through us. We will no longer deny spirit. Then we can really say that we are faithful, full of faith, acting and living spirit.

This is finding the jewel
in the molasses—finding
the spirit in all!

Finding The Jewel In The Molasses

Smile

Have you found time today to smile,
        your soul to play?
Have You for joy, sought and launched
        one rich smile of gladsome thought
upon Life's swift way?

Have You and smile already met
        for appreciation to beget?
Which styled into a song
        could right some wrong,
and erase regret.

Then you are invited, nay,
        commanded to smile and pray.
Smile, rise up and be free.
        God's Love commissioned thee
to smile, laugh and play.

Finding The Jewel In The Molasses

Choice

I don't remember where I first did hear
to be or not to be, that's the question.
It does not matter how it does appear.
I know that it is neither trend nor motion
because I listen to my inner voice,
No way can I be touched by any temptation.
To be or not to be, I made the choice.
I know now that it is "to be"
this life with many options.

You may activate your pursuance of
anything you want
and succeed.

So if it is not part of
your destiny,
you may not benefit from it.

Life is a learning process.
Life is a research project.

Surrender to your heart.
Do not question what is asked of you to do.
Act upon your heart's prompting.

Dare to risk.

Be totally free.

Humor

When the day moves in and out its track,
>with its ups and downs, I try to trace it back
by bringing into mind the caprice of the clown,
>to be able to see the humor of it all,
removes the frown and tension of my face.
>Suddenly, then I'm walking tall,
of darkness, no more trace.
>I find myself on the sunny side of the street,
and know I have my troubles beat.

Doubting and questioning always
interferes with the momentum.
Never, never, never stop the momentum.

Get rid of the training wheels
when you know how to ride.

Finding The Jewel In The Molasses

Wit

When, seemingly, all troubles come down,
  start smiling and reverse the frown.
And, even when troubles quest to stay,
  it signals for Faith, it's time to play.

Should I become subject to a nasty rumor,
  I respond to it with jest and humor.
No matter in life, I do or say,
  gossip will be there and try to stay.

With Faith, the blessing of my life,
  I know, through joy, I'll survive
with cheerfulness, happiness and wit,
  my heart full of light and always lit.

And, even if I get sometimes riled,
  I remember to give space to my inner child,
which, to negativity it says, "Nay!"
  And invites you all, come laugh and play.

The greatest toxin is created in
the doubting mind.

Questioning thinking or
doubting interferes with
the momentum of spontaneity
causing lack of assimilation of
brain chemicals, thus toxins.

When the mind becomes constipated,

the body follows.

Anxiety should be the energy
we utilize to go into action.
If you become anxious, get into motion
and express spontaneously.

Life without stress is death,

therefore play.

Relentless Love

Expression of Love's relentless power,
    Thou tamer of the human breast,
Thou saveth us in the gravest hour
    from pity, deep regret.
Revealer of the quest,
    Thou liberated us from assumed conditions,
transform the fire into light,
    bringeth forth true renditions,
of the mission and the plight.

Relentless Love,
    discoverer of magic in human breast,
wondrous strong,
    no longer with fears and doubts obsessed,
or with fault, or wrong,
    plying with the Healer's art,
Restorer of the broken heart,
    with thee, the answer of the plea,
We find the Truth that sets us free.

Life is a stage on which we are
acting out a drama; the problem
is that we like to make it a melodrama.

If you want to shine your light,

you first have to take in light.

To start expressing yourself as a jewel, you need to radiate from all your facets.

Non-Attachment

Surrounded by my possessions as far as I could see,
thinking of how much I had, not of what I could be.
Fearing that someone might take something away,
I could not move, attached, I must stay.

Dominated by all my wants and all my needs,
consumed by fear of loss, destroyed by greed.
Till suddenly, as through an act of God,
everything was lost, the whole lot.

It was gone and it set me free,
non-attached, to act upon what I could be.
None of the old remained, not even a fraction,
challenged by Spirit, I entered the Path of Action.

In order to become Non-Attached, we let go
of the dominant attachment and attach
ourselves to a higher need.

Non-Attachment is diving in with your
eyes wide open and reveling in the
situation with total awareness of what is
happening now and not in relation to old
dominating concepts, habits and
addictions.

Non-Attachment is acknowledging
responsibility to risk and live any
situation without impairment Knowing
that it is what you need right now.

How dare you call anyone an addict if you
are addicted to your own judgments.

Do not personalize

the past.

Say, "it happened,"

not, "it happened,"

to me

Worrying affects the thyroid by
strangulating and suffocating it.

So?

Since the thyroid metabolizes energy, it
impairs the flow.

Finding The Jewel In The Molasses

Awaken

Awaken to life's flowing river,
    the stream of sustenance from the Giver.
Awaken to the greening of the tree,
    its growth and strength endowed by Thee.
Awaken to all the flowers' beauty bloom,
    dispelling all the dark and gloom.
Awaken to the stillness of the reflecting lake,
    showing us thoughts of a divine make.
Awaken to the vastness of the sky,
    all clouds of sorrow drifting by and by.
Awaken to the rising sun in the east,
    preparing for a new life, a heavenly feast.
Awaken to the calling of the higher mind,
    providing Peace and Harmony for all humankind.
The resurrection, the freedom of the soul,
    is the awakening through which we become whole.

If you wake up in the morning,

you know you have more to learn.

Spontaneous articulation is making a joint
between the higher and the lower.
When the information of the Universe is
jointed with the local environment
without questioning, it is spontaneous
articulation.

Jump in and experience every situation spontaneously.

Sincerity

In this world with all its politics,
    its excessiveness and its frolics,
We are, nevertheless, all on a quest,
    to find and behold the truth, its best.

The sincerity that comes from within,
    that's where the joys of life begin.
Listen well to the inner voice you hear,
    And know to express that which is sincere.

Then, let it sound triumphantly,
    dismissing all adversity.
No longer will it be a test,
    But a reality, the answer to our quest.

If your love is based on being accepted,

there is no love.

You're unique, don't compare.

Recognize your oneness with mankind,

but be yourself and authentic.

Stay honest to yourself.

Give up the "me." Live in the Thou,

but be willing to take the consequences.

Rather than attempting to change the
environment;
Change the self and adapt to the
environment.

Finding The Jewel In The Molasses

Discover

When diving into the depth of my being,
  I explore the truth, demand the seeing.
The opening of the inner eye,
  listening to the distant cry.
The feeling of my inner craving,
  to know myself and, thus behaving
according to the message of my soul.

No longer lost, no longer dole.
  But freely giving and with zeal,
acting upon that what the soul reveal.
  No longer confused by worldly distraction,
now fully open for Heaven's satisfaction.

To Know the Power from above,
  the recipient of this, Eternal Love.
Then it is that I discover,
  in order to become the beloved,
I have to be the Lover.

As long as you have no self esteem or
self-worthiness, you are worrying.
Seeking approval or conformation is
worrying.

Please, please,

always be good to yourself.

Hate causes destruction

within the self.

There are no failures,

only experiences.

Discipline

When discipline's followed from outside world,
be sure in chaos you'll be hurled.
Following something one doesn't know,
will steer you away, blow by blow.

When discipline's followed from inside world,
in comfort and knowingness you'll be unfurled.
By following that which one knows,
gives insight into the cosmic flows.

Discipline, discipleship, for you to be
of the higher Self, for you to see.
The truth, source of your imagination,
fruitful joy, happiness and elation.

So follow, then, your inner Path,
preventing surely ignorance's wrath.
A disciple of the higher Self, The Thou,
will set you free and show you how.

Once questioning a thought, momentum
stops, stagnations start.

All questioning thoughts stagnate energy,
and toxify the brain.

Spontaneously express what you perceive.

Fear not,

be free and live in the present.

Set yourself free.

Our disguises are designed to hide the

truth from us and others:

self deception.

Always keep the amplitude high

by exciting and radiating.

Absorb not!

Look

"Look" direct your eyes in order to see
the future how good it will be.
"Look" for the path towards the light
guiding you when it shines clear and bright.
"Look" with the mind's eye into your heart;
it will show you the way from the start.
"Look" at your beauty and spiritual wealth,
the power to be harmonious in peace and health.
"Look" at all you can share and all you can give;
the more you see, the happier you will live!

One receives insights to act upon them,

not to store them up.

Only look to see how the experience is
helping you to learn and grow.
Always be totally aware.

If your mirror is foggy,

everything appears foggy.

If your mirror is crystal clear and you see

fogginess, it is in the other being.

Silence

After rising of the sun.
When daily labor has begun,
in the busy motion of the day,
It seems that sounds are here to stay.

But in the midst of all this noise,
there beckons to listen to the silent voice,
Always there and always near,
To point the way for us to hear.

Then after all the work is done,
the stars and moon replace the sun.
Then listen to the silence, the voice Divine,
to hear the truth, which is thine.

Every toxin starts in the brain, a thought
not followed up on.

Success does not come from outside measure but from internal feeling, and drives one to move on.

The Universe never waits for you. It is producing a zillion programs. But if we never turn on our set, we will miss the programs.

Listen

"*Listen*" to that still, inner voice
    letting you know there's always another choice.
"*Listen*" to that voice, quiet but clear,
    this power never gone but always here.
"*Listen*" what it is telling you now,
    not only when, but also how.
"*Listen*" it is beckoning for you to see
    where to go and how to be.

"*Listen*" to what the body needs most,
    so you can be its gracious host,
"*Listen*" to what is your mind and heart's desire,
    to what your soul insists to inspire.
"*Listen*" to that silent sound,
    heed it and you will be harmony bound.

All of the body is in the Mind.

Not all of the Mind is in the body.

It is always your choice.

Never be obedient to an external;

Be obedient to yourself

On the path of Love you acknowledge
yourself as the endowed authority.

You do not change your mind.

Allow your Mind to change you.

Grace

Help me to know my actions,
Help me to learn to forgive.
Before my heart breaks into fractions,
teach me my soul to live
in loving ways, by your grace.
Let me walk joyously
along the stream of life,
with a smile upon my face
that I will shine a radiant beam
into the darkness a ray of light.
So love will right the wrong,
and by your Grace and by your might,
You will awaken me into being with your song.

Empty thyself,

and I will fill thee.

Trust

and your emptiness will

fill with what you need.

One's best protection
is to be in harmony.

Only through radiance can you connect
with the paraconscious.

Empowerment

From higher source it came,
    the empowerment to change the light
into the fire, that feeds the flame
    to burn away all ignorance and fright,
and so filled my heart with Love
    all through empowerment from above.

By listening to the small inner voice
    I am enabled to understand the gift.
Permission to know and make a choice,
    to use the power and bend
with flexibility in order to give to others
    the love, the power to live.

Em-powerment is the energy in motion
with power.
Em-pirical is energy in motion
with fire.
Em-powerment is allowing others
permission to look at their own truth.

Radiance can only occur if it
is energy in motion, and for that,
momentum has to be maintained.

Finding The Jewel In The Molasses

Growth

When spirit descended from above to the below,
    with its love and compassion, it did bestow
all my attributes to bring to life,
    in this world full of need, full of strife.
By practice, I sure would learn
    that none comes free, one has to earn.
I'm grateful, what has been attained so far,
    and keep on reaching for the star.
Its twinkling light lets me know
    that, with every step, I will grow.

Never resist

and never fight changes.

Utilizing your hands
as jumper cables is the quickest way
to clear out energy blocks.

The key to the new education is to allow
freedom to express.

All acts against ourselves
and nature for acceptance will
cause trauma and disease.

Reap

There comes a glorious time, when we shall know,
    'tis harvest time, that we will reap what we did sow.
The soul then sees and hears
    the purpose of the moans and tears; and
by all the gathering of the sheaves,
    we see the growth, the fruit of fears and grieves.
Discover how we, in time, have changed,
    and wisdom, the flowers of knowing, arranged.
And walk together through life's barren fields,
    and sow together for next harvest's yields.
Sown in heart of hearts, hidden deep,
    are truth and love for us to reap.

Your power must be radiant and
continuous. The moment one doubt comes
in, you interfere and repress.

So?

At that moment toxins are created.

Every act of jealousy or hate is an
act of cellular suicide.
The body will destroy itself chemically.

To transcend belief systems,
one must transcend the need for approval
and value systems.

No one is going to change you.
You must change yourself.

Finding The Jewel In The Molasses

Harvest

Thanksgiving glowing in the harvest moon,
 announcing the winter coming soon.
Thanks are filling the ears
 for the labor and harvest we took part.
In our minds we find on file
 a harvest of love, joy and smile.
In our souls we did attain a gratefulness
 for Love, that will remain.

For strength in body, mind and soul, we give thanks,
 preparing us for nature's winter pranks.
Since winter will bring us life's new birth,
 we herald thanksgiving with gratefulness and mirth.

When you use your manure as fertilizer,

you are taking charge of your life.

Live miserably.
Die miserably.
As you sow,
so shall you reap.

Through activity,

we nourish.

Justice

The search is on for what's true and fair;
    no longer judgment, that's right and that's wrong.
Seeing and knowing the truth was always there.
    Divine justice, by its nature strong
transcends self righteousness, falsehood's pride.
    Born in loving, caring heart,
where no ignorance can hide,
    human fairness finds its start.
Human fairness is God's decree.
    To live a life that's true and fair,
be an example, but let others be.
    You are unique, no need to compare.

The Universe is holonomic:

the whole Law

Nothing in the universe is regressive.

The Universe is progressive by nature.

Never compare.

Experience the uniqueness and be

challenged by it.

Miracles

Many hours and days I have spent,
    maintaining my following of worldly trend.
Concerned by all the things of material kind,
    has rendered me practically blind
to all the miracles for me to see,
    provided in Nature in creation by thee.

Perplexed by all the noises around,
    I could not hear thy miraculous sound.
But now, my loving heart is appealing,
    to see and hear the miracles of healing.
I follow now my heart's voice, redirect my eye's aim,
    I am ready to act and my miracles to claim.

Intention:

putting tension into it that provides the

power to attain the purpose.

There is a cosmic conspiracy.
The conspiracy is not to keep us down,
but to waken us to grow.

As long as you need security for your
beingness, you will not experience the
order in your chemical chaos.

If a person is excited 48 hours a day,

one will not experience changes as disease,

but rather as evolutionary existence.

Eternal Love

Oh summer day, that ripens love's blossoms in an hour,
  oh, rosebud breast that frightens
my pale lips with it dower;
  to this Love's day in June,
drink I ... and it is noon.

How swift hours fly, love-laden,
  though we would stay them fast,
to bind for man and maiden,
  their first kiss with their last.
Even when I hold you tight,
  the roses fade, it is night.

One summer day,
  You chased the sleep hours away,
and in their stead,
  a heavenly feast of Love you speak,
timeless it runs;
  nor days nor nights,
nor rising setting suns,
  can mark its end,
For true Love richer grows,
  the more we spend.

You have to be intimate with yourself
before you can be intimate
with someone else.

The truth knows no words.
It radiates from your being.

Currency has to be activated into motion,
to create interest. It needs to be invested to
flow, to create a current.

When you get,

you need to be-get!

Vision

I have a vision for all to be seen
  of a world so peaceful, it ever has been.
I have a vision of a beautiful dove,
  spreading its wings and message of love.
I have a vision of people and how it'll be,
  that they will live in harmony, happy and free.

I have a vision of the planet Earth in splendid health
  with industrious people now sharing their wealth.
I have a vision of friendship and clearness of mind
  where all have shelter -- leave homelessness behind.
I have a vision of a life where Spirit will reign,
  the end of all wars and actions of Abel and Cain.

I have a vision of sisters and brothers
  together, they are, working and living as equals,
with compassion its star.
  I have a vision of the nineties to be,
a renewal of the Spirit,
  integrity its decree.

Past history matters not.

Materialize not the past.

The new education is to bring forth
sun-like radiant students,
reflecting the now, not the moon-like
mirror images of the past.

Follow the Law of Transformation.

Allow change to take place.

Take the risk.

The universe only supplies you with the

energy so you can utilize it

and return it fulfilled.

Finding The Jewel In The Molasses

Reflection

Looking deep into the lake of the mind,
    there were no reflections of what lies behind,
Only images of the present, of the now,
    forcing the knowing towards the brow.
That, what I live, I need to love,
    with constant help from the Light above.
Shining upon the days which lie ahead,
    reflecting the path, to earn the spiritual spread.
Looking deep into the lake of my mind,
    I now know that Love, Health and Happiness
will bind.

No two experiences can be the same.

So?

Move on and experience the new situation
without the trauma of the old.

I cannot have brand new, pure experiences
unless I completely die out
of the old experiences.

If you can't do it out of Love,

bother not.

Love must be expressed wholly and freely.

Hence we know from the heart,

act from the heart.

Finding The Jewel In The Molasses

Shine

After moonlight, comes sunrise and singing sea,
    life's awakening call to me.
Freedom, Truth and Light,
    my tools for the work divine.
This day, to fulfill my plight,
    reflections of my soul will shine.

Shining, they give my thoughts their wing,
    inspire the happy songs I sing.
With tones sounding crystal clear,
    awaken courage, dispel all fear.
Envision all light with rays so fine,
    reflections of my soul, they shine.

Give value to the tool

and know when and how to use it.

Don't log with a butter knife and then

complain that others are doing better.

Open your tool box.

What we see,

we need to transcend.

Our only duty is to shine.

Be the process,

without attachment to the outcome.

Light

Come on, come, ye children of the Light,
    wake up and start shining bright.
Your task is clear and right at hand,
    to take care of your beings and your land.
Let us carefully remove the curtain
    from all that's vague or uncertain.
Discover that the time is here
    to make changes, ban all fear.
With courage, lighten up, prepare to give
    Your radiant self to all that is meant to live.

When we hold on to form
we become non-radiant, molasses like.
When we express spontaneously
from the heart, we radiate like the sun.

The Sun provides its energy

without judgment on how

it should be used.

Never accept anything; only acknowledge.

When you acknowledge anything,

you take responsibility for new change.

Never be satisfied with the moment,

but be content with it.

Contentment says, "That is where I need

to be and the best I can do at the moment."

Finding The Jewel In The Molasses

Dance

When upon life's rocky pathways you walk,
    shadowy tribulations do stalk.
When all things seem to hinder your ploy,
    look deep in your heart, where you store your joy.

Unmask your suffering and take your chance,
    come on, join the happiness, let's dance!
Sail your soul's ship, dancing on waves of the cosmic sea,
    fly with the birds, on wings of love, to set you free.

Roam nature graciously with the antelope and deer,
    conquering all troubles, dispelling all fear.
Become a radiant one, the way to advance,
    come on, join with happiness, let's dance!

We are not here to learn information or
knowledge; we are here to dance.
Explore the Cosmic information, and
dance with it spontaneously.

Give up the idea

why is this happening to me?

Only look to see how the experience is

helping you to learn and grow.

When you climb a mountain you must
come down again before you can go
up the next one.

So?

The key is

don't lose the momentum

when you go down, by attaching to

any part of the experience.

Keep the momentum going.
Go full speed into the depths
to carry you through the next high.

The answer to the question

Why me, God?

Because I needed the changes that this

situation will provide.

Rhythm

A new rhythm is about to begin,
   creating harmony, disbanding sin.
With the cadence of an angel's hark,
   rhythmic movement of light and dark.

Like the ticking of a clock,
   like the migration of a flock,
Life's movement in perfect harmony,
   that brings the truth which sets us free.

Be neither submissive nor aggressive.

Both take energy.

Be harmonious.

Use all of your gears.

Don't stay in first.

Health is not a static state.

Finding The Jewel In The Molasses

Vibration

The Universe in its divine creation,
  with all its energy transforming in the round,
its motion with continuous vibration,
  playing its instrument with light and sound.

Oh, Creative Force of my life and destiny,
  let me play my instrument with yours in harmony
that I will recognize and respond to my relations,
  by being in tune and resonant with your vibrations.

To fulfill my co-creative part,
  I will use the stirring of my heart.
I will listen to your vibrational call,
  and be attuned with the All.

E-Motions are the energy in motion.

All else are demotions.

Repressed feelings are demotions.

When we are demoted,

we miss the pro-motion.

Therefore maintain the energy in motion.

Lower energy can never enter
into a field of higher energy, without being
changed into the higher;
the lower cannot affect the higher.

Garbage out;

Garbage in.

I cannot be afflicted until I fail

to radiate.

De-liberation imprisons the light.

Finding The Jewel In The Molasses

Reverence

When I look at the vast, blue sky,
    the sun at midst and clouds drift by.
At the horizon, the mountains arise,
    surrounded by forests and flowers' surprise.
The sounds of the babbling waters I hear,
    it is then, that I know, it is Thou I revere.

When I look at the eyes in a newborn's face,
    the starry sparks revealing thy grace
of innocence, wisdom and truth from above,
    my heart inspires with the rapture of love.
Removing the doubts and anxious fear,
    it is then, that I know, it is Thou I revere.

Any spontaneous act is a spiritual act
and the expression of Universal Truth.

Consciousness is an inherent
quality of energy.

Never again look at a person's form
without exploring their soul and energy,
to perceive the whole person.

Raise your amplitude to transmit higher
and higher ideals. You can become
multidimensional in conscious awareness
like the holonomic Universe.

Humility

Humbly, I will build for my spirit a house,
　　a house with a garden fair.
Modest shall be its dimensions,
　　befitting the humble tenant there.

No glory shall fill its portals,
　　nor fame rear its altar within.
The door to my house shall be lowly,
　　earthly and homely, like sin.

Yet pillars of strength and beauty,
　　around and about it I'll raise.
These shall uplift my spirit,
　　and music shall voice its praise.

Broad and deep be its windows,
　　for the sweep of the heavens above.
And, the lustrous fragrance of meadows,
　　the limitless power of Love.

Disease:

a compilation of situations and conditions
that we claim ownership of, but are not
willing to pay property taxes for.

There is no ownership, there is only
temporarily utilization of form.
Drop all ownership rights.

Real E-state (real estate)
If you want to own the property
and claim it,
don't squawk about the taxes.

The only way to heal is to transmute and set free. Liberate that what you imprisoned.

Happiness

The spiritual journey we started,
     a vision quest, a daring pursuit
for happiness where grief and sorrow parted,
     to make room for peace, joy and good.
Finding that space in our radiant hearts,
     filled with faith, hope and love.

Not craving for worldly rewards,
     but looking for blessings of happiness from above;
going forward, leaving behind our past.

Sharing our visions, our hopes, our dreams,
     our happiness on the waters of life we cast,
to uplift the fellow travelers we meet on our way;
     letting them know, our happiness is here to stay.

The truest gift would be the
knowing of how to enjoy life.

The doors of pain and happiness
are the same door.

Never do anything

to get results.

Never, never, never,
never want to be accepted.
The price is too high.

Prosperity

Let us live long and live well!
    All other life is empty and vain.
Those that live long they can tell
    that their prosperity is of heavenly gain.

Let prosperity be our wisdom's well;
    those who think prosperity must live it too!
They are the wisest who can tell
    how they loved and lived to speak the true.

Let us be what we seem, live our creed,
    keep our heart as the torch divine.
Be what we pray, to be made indeed,
    let the Master's prosperity be thine.

Fill up your life with what will last;
    prosper with the moments as they go.
The prosperity above, when all this is past
    is the ripened fruit of life below.

Look for sources, not re-sources.

Search instead of re-search.

Always look for the source.

Leave off the prefix re.

Always count your blessings,

not your symptoms.

Celebrate the gain,

not the loss.

Finding The Jewel In The Molasses

Wealth

Enhanced within a treasure chest, your soul,
　　born unto this world, this earth,
You came to share your gifts,
　　to let that be your goal.

A vision quest, to see what's there to offer,
　　a joyful state, a touch, a smile.
All gifts from the Godly coffer,
　　given out of love, none are vile.

Let love for all be your strife,
　　your richness and your wealth.
Giving purpose, value to your life,
　　awarding you with health.

The concept of life
is the concept of
constant transformation.

It is our fears of and resistance to change
that causes disease.
Fear of change means lack of spontaneity.

Your mission is to serve,

not to deserve.

The grand national product of the USA
is Dis-Ease.

Finding The Jewel In The Molasses

Power

Standing at the shore of life's sea,
  I ponder about that what was, is and will be.
Observing the changes of the tide,
  waves rolling in and out,
knowing that its motion I need to abide.
  To release the power, diminish the doubt,
broaden my awareness, expand my range,
  with faith in the future to be.
Overcoming the fear of change,
  by setting myself free, I no longer cower.
No longer fear's slave, I obey God's innate power,
  and become life's sailor, courageous and brave!

The more non-attached,

the more involved you become,

the more risk you take.

There is no evolvement
without involvement.

Let your symptoms be the alarm clock
to awaken you to the changes taking place.

Most people want to change the body,

but don't want to change the Self.

Ecstasy

When toiling on this path of our ploy,
  receiving as fruit the state of joy,
Enthusiasm was our start,
  and joy which filled the heart.
Became the source of blazing ecstasy,
  awakening us to our divinity,
No longer flee or fight.
  Nor shadows of the past blocking our light,
Enabling us to move and see,
  a fruitful life awaits, with ecstasy.

Contained Ecstasy

is the highest

constant motion of energy.

The Law of Resonance:

whatever one transmits, one receives.

The Law of Attraction:

garbage out - garbage in.

Finding The Jewel In The Molasses

Whole

When I found myself roaming life's worldly way,
   I got confused and went astray.
By giving importance to the found worldly part,
   I lost sight of the giving of my heart
Constantly reminding me of the calling of my soul,
   to search for all, but behold the Whole.
To recognize that the worldly strife,
   estranged me from my Spiritual Life.
Slowly now, awakening to my higher me,
   I start to perceive what I need to see.
The way is clear, the way of the soul:
   To combine the parts and act upon the whole.

Trauma is misinterpretation of any
experience because we fail to respond
to the whole picture.

The electropotentials of the whole mind
become the chemistry of the
brain and body.

One must become excited

to find a higher need.

Imagine

Imagine you found wealth in the gold of the sunset,
  beauty in moon and star.
Imagine you felt grace in the bloom of the lily,
  strength in the hills afar.
Imagine experiencing joy in the carols of morning,
  laughter in labor at noon,
Hope in the hush of evening,
  light in the midnight gloom.
Imagine you saw love in the heart of woman,
  wisdom and power in man.
Building and shaping together,
  life for its deathless span.

Finding The Jewel In The Molasses

Radiant

You were radiant today,
    so full of loving laughter.
Your radiant spirit leaped to play,
    while mine came shining after.
Now that you are far away,
    I am still radiant today.
Though I feel radiant enough for tomorrow,
    I will keep on shining throughout the night,
To overcome darkness and all sorrow,
    bringing beaming happiness,
With my Radiant Light.

We get to know more about the Universe
by our radiance, by resonance.

The greatest sin

is that we do not shine out.

We do not shine out indiscriminately;

we concentrate on a specific.

Life is meant for just

pouring out our energy.

It falls upon whatever it falls upon.

Touch

Know how blessed you are,
>   to have the gift to touch from close by or afar.
To touch, there are many ways,
>   as many as the Sun has rays.
To touch with a loving word,
>   can strike in the heart a tender chord.
To touch with the eye a spark lasting awhile
>   erases the tears, restores the smile.
A touch with the hand to let them know
>   you're always there, wherever they go.
A touch of light out of the depth of your soul,
>   can make them happy and whole.
So go out ready to touch;
>   It will reach where it is needed so much.

Merely Radiate and be.
Give not thought to
outcomes and results.

Never tell anyone what you're going to do,

Just respond, act, be.

The Universe is for-giving
and not for-getting.

Relationship

One morning I woke up on this earth,
  to start a life-long trip,
A journey of discovery,
  to find my worth,
By giving and receiving love,
  in unconditional relationships.
I've traveled far,
  I've traveled near,
In pursuit of happiness,
  peace and harmony.
Experiencing sadness, joy,
  courage and fear.
Now I've found all I need,
  in my relationship with thee.
I've stopped my travel,
  and my strife.
And now enjoy glorious kinship,
  with all life!

Love to share your energy.

Share your love.

Every time you express,

you teach that expression,

and you learn by it.

The only way I can give Love

is to have sufficient self-awareness.

The only prayer for anyone is to send
all of the Love you have
in the form of Light.

Finding The Jewel In The Molasses

Always

I want to lay hold of rainbow's end,
    and track it upward over the bend
to where its magical colors blend.
    In the sheen of the infinite sea
To always have faith in thee.

I want to see in the violet eyes
    the mystic glory of sunset skies,
and share the ages' stark surprise,
    such health it then would be,
for always there for me to see.

I want to know whence truth is sown,
    from what fair flower is beauty blown,
where justice build her royal throne.
    For Universal sway
truth always is there to stay.

Finding The Jewel In The Molasses

And who it is that lights the stars,
    the planets - Venus, Neptune, Mars.
Who lifts the night's strong prison bars,
    lets in the golden day,
be it so always, as it may.

I want to win my heart this world,
    its every banner and flag unfurled.
As from the Creator's hand it whirled
    on its ageless quest,
for always to show its best.

Share the passion of human-kind,
    the power of will and mind,
delve to life's inmost realms to find,
    their light and Love,
as is always and always in the above.

As a human being, you have all divine
possibilities at your fingertips.
Don't pray to acquire something
you already possess.

There is a reason for everything,

but we don't always have to

know the reason.

Don't ask the creative intelligence
to do anything for you.
It has done everything already.
It's up to you to recognize that
and use it!

The world of things

is conceptual reality;

infinite reality is perceptual.

If you don't access the infinite,

you can't make changes in the finite.

Index

A

B

C

D

E

About The Author

Jack Schwarz, a pioneer in the education health field has gained worldwide recognition for his work. He is the president of the Aletheia Institute, which he founded in 1958, and has been a subject, researcher, and consultant at major biomedical and life science research centers in the United

States and abroad. Results of tests performed on Jack document his abilities to self-regulate many psychophysiological processes.

Finding The Jewel In The Molasses is the latest in a series of books in which Jack Schwarz explores the dynamics of health education, always with an emphasis on energy and self-regulation. He is dedicated to educating others in self-health and awareness, and bringing together research on health and human energies.

For further information on Jack Schwarz and the Aletheia Institute, contact Aletheia Institute515 N.E. 8th Street, Grants Pass, OR 97526, (541) 479-4855.

Don Ingram

Don Ingram is an educator. He has worked with children in elementary schools for 39 years, working with children from ages 8 to 12. Most of his career has been in Oregon, but he has also taught in the Bahama Islands, Bahrain and in Germany. He has always considered developing the human being as a person to be more important than mere knowledge.

Don Ingram first met Jack Schwarz in 1981 in Ashland, Oregon. Since that time he has changed his life. Having been in public education for 56 of his 62 years, he was trained to believe in someone else's authority. When he began to study with Jack, he found out that learning is the creative act of the learner. It was no longer good enough to hear information and be able to believe it was true, and then consider one was educated. To follow the materials presented at Aletheia H.E.A.R.T. Institute, Don had to go to work and actually do the learning and growing.

Since 1981 Don was a part of a small group of

educators that started a small school dedicated to the concept that the child has to initiate his/her own learning and has to learn based on his/her own effort. The small school, Amity Creek, in Bend, Oregon is an ongoing magnet school where the children are presented with the ideas of Jack Schwarz and given the opportunity to learn the responsibility necessary to grow into autonomous beings with skills that will provide them with life long learning.

Don not only works with students in the school, but also works with staff, parents and beginning teachers to help them understand the important part each person plays in his or her own development.

After 15 years of study, including a four-year internship, Don Ingram has discovered that the greatest gift a master can bestow upon a student, is the gift of autonomy and authority through knowing.

Aletheia Institute
Since 1958

The Aletheia Foundation dedicates itself to increasing harmony, health and happiness in the world by bringing forth integrative changes in individuals. Our programs, supported through research, educate people in practical and effective methods for achieving optimal health through self-regulation and self-management.

It is our utmost desire to promote innovative health education by blending experiential, educational, and research results with existing lifestyles and modes of health education. We wish to network with other individuals, medical, educational, and research professionals within our community, the nation and the world for the betterment of humankind.

Our programs with Jack Schwarz:

P.H.T.

The personal health training program educates people from all walks of life about how various forms of energy and self-regulation relate to their individual health and well-being. The following trainings are included: voluntary controls, human energies, autogenic feedback, nutrition, mind-body assessment, self-massage and biotonics.

INTERNSHIP PROGRAM

Specialized training emphasizing self-regulation and the human energies.

ACCELERATING CENTER WORKSHOPS

Workshops given on the human energy centers, diet and nutrition, human energy intensive, transcending into knowingness annual intensive, exploring the paraconscious, energy in motion with light, color and sound, and super-teaching. Plus many more workshops and conferences throughout the year.

National and International workshops given throughout the year.

Many tools for self-discovery—books, tapes and videos, plus the ISIS Instrument.

For further information, newsletter and tools for study on Jack Schwarz and Aletheia contact:

The Aletheia Institute
P.O. Box 2400
Mendocino, CA 95460
Voice (707) 937-0602
Fax (707) 937-0624
E-Mail: aletheia@mcn.org
Website: http://www.magick.net~/aletheia

Give a gift of self-health education and compassion

ORDER FORM

Yes, I want _____ copies of *Finding The Jewel In The Molassas* at \$14.95 each, plus \$5.00 shipping per book. Allow 30 days for delivery.
❏ check/money order enclosed
Charge my ❏ Visa   ❏ Mastercard

Name _____

Organization _____

Address _____

City/State/Zip _____

Phone (   ) _____

Card # _____ Exp. date _____

Signature _____

Make your check payable and return to:
Aletheia Institute
P.O. Box 2400
Mendocino, CA 95460